Ian U Lockaby's *Defensible Space/if a crow*— hums in the steady silver rhythms
of a hymn whose feeling has gotten in, desires to get out, and once out — "I
don't know" — the pleasure burns out. Or, chooses again. These poems evoke
the feeling of a constant, cold, damp, summer of the Pacific Northwest. A
hazy herbarium of plants, seeds, and vegetables. A recurring whale, waxing
neotropical poetics as black wings, ash, the remains of what came prior. In
love, a reason — "I wanted to make one rhyme with you" — recast as the
smoldering of a poet's quire. Sometimes we must burn the thing before we
finish it, begin again. It is devotion, aftershocks stirred deep within the fiery
Earth, an unrelenting quiet devotion of tremors inside these icy roots.

—fahima ife, author *Septet for the Luminous Ones*

Entering this manuscript was like entering a spell. The work immediately
opened to a landscape where "a black ice cube pressed / against the grain of
the sun" mirrors the crow which hangs like a specter in the atmosphere of this
book. The measured line sometimes pitches into lyric scattered across the page
and at other times aggregates, pulls itself in tightly as the speaker explains that
"Inside of this life ... / is another life/ I cannot claim." This poet's embrace of
a stuttering utterance is masterful as the interstitial pause dominates a page so
that we are caught up in the trepidation of a beingness that "bursts   into a
thousand fledglings / ... " The book's refrain takes us, through the conditional
made image — If, a crow— from the tucked in voice of a naturally lugubrious
landscape to a joy that is ordered, numbered, and measured, that is, joy that
is joy precisely because of the limitations of joy. I feel blessed to have met this
book but more, to have experienced a poetics brave enough to embrace the
unbearable as transformative.

—Ruth Ellen Kocher, author of *Archon/After*, judge's citation for the
Omnidawn Poetry Chapbook Contest

Written in the excluded middle between if and then, this gorgeously anarchic serial poem offers not alternative logic, but an alternative to logic. Persisting as "a threat to the structure," where "the structure" is private property or lyric propriety or anthropocentricism, *Defensible Space/if a crow*— performs a way of being textual that's meant "to true/the obligation" to other species while being true to human experience too. Beloved and lovelorn, ecstatic and addicted, outdoors and indoors, we join crows, whales, and termites – air, water, and earth – and reader we fly, swim, and chew through this elemental poetics whose finely tuned lines intertwine human and more-than-human lives and hungers.

—Brian Teare, author of *Poem Bitten by a Man*

Defensible Space/

if a crow—

Cover art by Clara DeWeese.
cover art title: "Linnae Slash Pile"

Cover design by by Ian U Lockaby
Interior design by Sophia Carr and Laura Joakimson
Cover typeface: Copperplate Gothic and Didot
Interior typeface: Century Gothic and Garamond Premiere Pro

Library of Congress Cataloging-in-Publication Data

Names: Lockaby, Ian U, 1989- author.
Title: Defensible space / if a crow— / Ian U Lockaby.
Description: Oakland, California : Omnidawn Publishing, 2024. | Summary:
"Considering how we might detox from old languages, systems, and modes
of life, Ian Lockaby's poems seek out new forms of interconnectivity and
possibility, finding the energy of emerging worlds along the edges of
ruins. This collection poses questions of how to thrive in aftermaths,
suggesting that attempts at absolute knowledge are less powerful than an
embrace of the unknown. Throughout these poems, Lockaby uses crows as a
model for dynamic adaption and creative entanglement with the world and
with language, finding "defensible space" for new lyrical syntax amid
shifts and desolation: "Everywhere a burning root system. Everywhere, a
root fire crowing off the splayed tail feathers of a crow." Defensible
Space / if a crow— looks towards a reintroduction of fire into wilds and
wilds into our lives, taking the unknown of an "if" as the base from
where we can build life"-- Provided by publisher.
Identifiers: LCCN 2024013879 | ISBN 9781632431592 (trade paperback ;
acid-free paper)
Subjects: LCGFT: Poetry.
Classification: LCC PS3612.O2464 D44 2024 | DDC 811/.6--dc23/eng/20240328
LC record available at https://lccn.loc.gov/2024013879

Published by Omnidawn Publishing, Oakland, California
www.omnidawn.com
10 9 8 7 6 5 4 3 2 1
ISBN: 978-1-63243-159-2

Defensible Space /

if a crow—

IAN U LOCKABY

OMNIDAWN PUBLISHING
OAKLAND, CALIFORNIA
2024

Contents

if a crow—

then a black ice cube pressed
against the grain of the sun

while the afternoon mugs drop
pattering spoils of a milk'd black coff-

-in the over grown carpets
lay   a caffeinated belly bitter against
the sleep against the damn

bright   slipping away.   if a crow—
remembers you,

by what:

Something   growly
in the vanilla leaf—

don't   dawdle now

it's plenty late.

A Way to Tell

You're learning a lot
     of sad useful things

upon the leaves of this awful summer—

            this book is
great—how it can make you
hear different

layers of it amplified in the stacked noise
     of the striated river, at different times

you've grown and used
different times—   You've learned to keep

thyme with each
of them, stacked and riveted
        to your ribcage now

And every time you stand, I try to

     stay still—to be
located inside of the ways I hear

At the upper edges
of the sages there

becomes something less sage
     than a turbid, herbal air

Under our hands,
     on the tablecloth the mountain is
running towards the city—

In the air above it is
little attention to these
maps:

cirque—medial moraines—andesite
the cold lavas—

Defensible space i

Maybe I will detox like the forest. Maybe I will detox like the dead. (even breathing that smoke now—how will it ever rid me of itself). The smoke off the crow. The smoke off the crow that tells of that fire in the forest, the burning lung the charred birds were breathed from. The must of broiled fir resins trapped in the embering feather down of their young.

At Trillium Lake

There is nausea on the shelves
        of A.'s grandmother

The eve of it A traveler
        who hasn't been here since
she was bedded down
in asylum   for softening

in the violet inconsistencies
        of mind
but who once set out from here—
mornings she'd take on
        mountaintops   alone

at night tender away
whichever worn page
                between five tongues
        she moored
                a distant   hunger to

Now cold quail climb windows
inside the coldest room
                in the house where
        most of the old machines
made up   for making fire—

We sleep aloft the threat
     of three of them
          anymore   sweat
through every night

Wanting and wanting
     but too hemmed in
by cold fever damp
        to every side of us

the trees   darken

raindrop drag through sappy
               fur filters
by   gravity waiting round the roots

A picnic basket full

of the names you've had for the herbs
　　　　in your food— *bad, good, uncontrollably-laughing-*
with-a-mouthful

A blackberry vine growing up through

　　　　the wicker bottom
of everything

Songbirds Mysteriously Dying

Inside of this life—

is another life
I cannot claim

the cicadas' hum
distracts the intelligence

of dogs,

cicadas hum and
mysteriously kill

songbirds—a panic
takes in the internet

birding groups
arguing over whether

to offer the birds water—

throw it in the trees
instead, they say

outside of one's reason
is another life

A lupine mash   boiled in the high sun
          for spirit   to pour over   the rose

seeds   risen to the rim   of the semi-annual

triggering—   bur owing facial tics   triggering

in   the deer   tracks

burs   two-deep skin cells
                                        pruned off

trails   away   ticking hips— lit

an arms aflame

if a crow—

a manic feather
copulated with—

when the weather   terns
        black fetters

cherry juice seeping from
the living   ground

under the weight   of ev'ry
 step a way   thru autum

'

Once a whale

ate   a   crow

it was   the meeting

of the loud dark   sky
and the quiet   many cathedrals

of the sea.

The whale belly   is

my belly   is
our belly

is   the quiet   cathedrals

full   of belly silks

I taste   a sulking crow   in the season

I devour many   mediocre

specimens

of

us

myself

Summer Where We

Deemed the strawberries unsaleable,
asked the butcher what bones

    hold the paper up— what bones
    in the red pepper red

paper bones— stack a pair
of pears and again then
to make a pair of a pair

      of pears
      and so on, just like
      us, all in our houses, paired up

But how do people—
hold up—?
All those paper bones—

      All summer was
    crows overhead, language
   breaking apart in my hands

The hips rose up the
        river chutes Shuttling

in   new terrains   grange

So quick   we're   semi-rooted— bitterly

burred—   a bur chap melody   chant
a tic's bad dream

To quit the smoke—

       a chalice of rose seeds
for breakfast—

       panting over it

if a crow—

      then a crow
in every window
\#   \#   full
                w ith nerve
\#   \#

Then
      all the c c c r rows
                    in only

          one window
            ` ` ` `
           ` ,,,,,,,,, `
            ` ` ` `
              suddenly

a blast of cold green
                     a furnace
                     outside

      clinkkkk k. k.   k
               of cooling

metal
      falling into the room

                 if a crow—
enters
      upon you   then

                 ‘

      the crow lands.

Another crow lands
          nearby

And bursts   into

'

a thousand

fledglings

``

``

`''' `

,

if a crow—
    then a crow

        I don't know

What it is
                a word has
    gotten into me

            what   I need

to get—   out—   out—

to get—   out—   out—

get it out—   out —

                        out of me—

'

,

Forecast

Not to be what one has
been but that

I can only have been what
I was
         (and so on—)

A banana in your fist in a
climate of catastrophe

séance of coffee sap and
stone   (the air is

cold here, even in summertime)

and it was summertime, it was cold,
it's snowing ash—

The best thing to have happened

to my lifestyle is
my lifestyle (which practically ate

the moth, as it landed on this page)

Are there plenty of places

for you to rest in the sun, moth?
(you choose me)

You are the second-best thing
to have happened to my life

(you choose me, again and again)

A crow grows a quivering tumor of feathers. It acts as a quiver of feathers—not for being bowed—but admired. Suddenly it breaks a beak and wings its way. The sun is smaller than the kidney stone of a fig.

'

The low black wings of a low sky machine. A low sky a machinery of mood.

Of black wings moving in a frenzy of black fish. In a low prey. Is a low pray.

Is magnificent and moody the only way towards prey.

The fish a frenzy so magnificent and moody like a machinery of black wings.

A low sky machine.

If the magnificence is fish. Then the machinery a mood. Therefore a black wings.

Black wings its way across your temperature.

If a crow, it's ambergris—

i.

        I wanted to make one rhyme with you.
        Lambent greys under the toilet skies, you—
        So long I am here to terrify myself with my tinyness.
        If it wasn't any trouble, it was all another drink.
        And if the rhyme wouldn't want with you,
                               it'll take itself back.

ii.

        I'm summering in the bathroom stall,
        memorizing sanitation law, tide tables of the toilet seas.
        I'm little enough to sea-fare. But when I try to
        flush the big apparent crow, that I might ride its weight down
        ward and out (towards autumn, the quiet cathedrals)—the
        body of the bird won't fit, and the tides come back that night
        whale-waked, a harvest wake. Could it take itself back? As the
        waking wants with you.

iii.

        Days later, the two bodies—crow
        and whale—stank together in a flesh-bog
        unison never replicated. To think of the possible
        pairs of flesh, feather, fiber never yet found dueting rot.
        What could it do for our senses to enjoy them?
        Or the perfume possibilities in the bile duct of the crow.

iv.

        In the terrible season, fledgling crows
        bountied dead upon the lawns—land-fallen
        ambergris struck low with tinnitis, down before first flight.

Now for our profit. If I tried to make this rhyme, it would say: of all the crows buried at sea, whatever happened to your plastic dolly, your marionette nose, the garbage pails in which you collected your plastics, marked with that occult triangle made you to believe in the myth: that whatever went in would be churned back in—to our tide of things— our tide of things—our tide of things—our tide of things—

but they dumped it into the sea.

Amiss

In the middle of
the street is everyone

you know. You
stand on the side-

walk,
missing them.

They begin to
spread out

around a neighbor-
hood, looking for

the cat you lost
as a child. You

don't remember its
name, but they

all seem to—
all calling out:

*Rain! Rain, don't go
away—*

*you're a cat and I
miss you and you're*

gone.

'

In the middle of the
street is the cat you

lost as a child. You
used to miss him—

but you don't any-
more. It begins to rain

but the cat doesn't
move, he just stares at

you, wide-eyed, as rain
washes the morning

dew from the back
of his ears.

You think of who
you were the day you

lost that cat. You
can remember how

your ears felt—all
burning and blood

but you cannot
remember the feeling

behind your heart
that day, anymore.

You speak to it—

*You're a cat,
and I miss you, and*

you're gone.

'

My heart

stands now in the
middle of the street.

It's starting to rain
again. Behind its ears,

the morning dew.
Sometimes it is so

lonely, being with
what you thought

you'd forgotten.
I hear everyone I

know, hollering
in the distance.

My heart jumps

up and walks away.

Defensible space ii

Maybe I will detox in the forest. Maybe I will detox when I'm dead. (even this carcinogen huff, fogging the summer sun, going mean genes in the farm's hands, an offering of ipecac against the tomato harvest—as if that old root solution might wrench the ash cough out of). The smoke through which the crow flies descended into and all about me. Everywhere a burning root system.

Everywhere, a root fire growing off the splayed tail feathers of a crow.

Cispus under the tansy swales—

       I wanted you   to find me   like a cat littered can with a .22 eye

in the mineral hazes // Cowlitz
                 up the fireweed fuse

slung up towards an untenable
skyline   in the breeches of

our settlement //   Encamps at
the highest reach of our cata-strophe

where   you can't breathe for
the thin bearings one's allowed

on themself (head off-
kilter for collision with   the fine fuse line of horizon— a weedy fuse line
of horizon sizzling in

the mineral hazes of larger fires to the east

A tea: weedy teases

       wet us
           down
                salving

           some soaked limbs   anti-
     cipate
some of the   our

a morass   in how   to find

homes in the logic

         of arson

           a nurse tree
               mega

       old mass, a limbing

I left because I needed to arrive. Always trying to arrive is one way to seldom do. An ever-arriving coincident with a failure to recognize it, the air of our heads conditioned to miss the particles we land on, over and over, this progress.

I left summer because fall was one way to fall away. It got cold, surfaces came unstuck. Carrying tobacco flowers in a glass jar grown from seed I'd been saving for years. I would smoke the flowers. I would save a few seeds, willing particles to land on. I would might then.

Carry one cigarette from the garden up the pass—

An empty packet of
         Regulator Extracts //   Hi-THC, Hi-Deltas—
at the gravel pull-off   over the runoff chute to

the mountain spring ditch, where we

swam naked in the plastic water bottle company's

water. They want to eat all the water, they said—
there will be nothing left but thirst and that's fine

                                                    fibers
explode in the glass, the windshield meets the weed-
dense wind—

Ghost bent over a down log   shiny bum
glowing bristly in the sun in the sum of the tasty ditch
the tansy crotch   O how the extracts hit— o how

    Some of this is   unbearably

what is

        a year ago, anymore—

A balsam root pointing down
         the palm of the   our hand

seconds

of one year—

        in the palm of the other:
a fist   still held in a fist   behind its own back

Refusal

I consented to
stone after stone

in the terrible
season till

it made
a riverbank

and the riverbank made
a sleeping form

upon which all
the rosehips were past

and now you are sleeping
drunk on a bed of them—

pressing them to dry
any way

that the forest
fire behaves

like liquid
down slopes above you is

what's been made—

The windowsill is hollowing itself. Stiff little mounds of sawdust coming up through the white paint. Tunnel-flex spills through the sill and I am wondering how long I can watch the termites progress before I am obligated to tell the landlord. Can the window be falling out loose in its socket, can the inside know the outside, can I hang the lords loose in the land's socket—

My only true obligation is threats to the landlord—

To map the routes through the windowsill before they give way to the will of the structure, swallowed to the belly of it. The concept of the structure is hungry for the cross-grains. For all that opposes it.

To name the termite settlement in my windowsill, fairly. What to call their settlement before a nuisance, an infestation trickling down into the economy of a landlord's headache—that which is to be eradicated in the interest of the structure.

What to name the termite town before a threat to the structure. So that it may survive as a threat to the structure.

if a whale once ate a termite

if an   echo-

logically plus rumor equals nothing
 lodges in you   like

          a termite
's eaten your whole house, there   for
uncomplicating   the maps:

a whale belly had   become your home

and   how to live

          inside a structure which

ate the threat

                    to the structure

if a crow—

in dialogues with a
whale—   how do you
speak with

a word in your mouth—

lichen it's having   a word
  with you

as you chew your molars
with its teats,

  you are gorgeous
with questions—

What flavor
    in the silks

I wash the   flavor
          in   the   silks

'

A whale calve   grown swimming in

the   billowy   echo   of
         crow v voicings s s

in the marble giant

           whale belly cathedral.

I   wash   the whale

with silks in the

          season's

      whale   belly   sinks

If a crow— no, termite. Winged it's

That the ashen crow might like to eat but the ash and crow can't eat, for its
lodge in the windowsill, dwelling in precipice—cocked in the threshold.
At the edge of our dwelling: a nuisance and a pest against the interest of
the structure. Crowdwelling at the fringe of our consumption patterns,
pattering at the edges of ways(te) we travel. There at the threshold,
                                                          thriving on the
                                                          heart of us.

If the crow thrives on what
gathers at the edge of us, is

What gathers at the edge of us is
                              where the heart of us, it's

if a crow—

then a smother-colored

saint,
iridescing like a
           tire fire with
                     one eye
   on the traffic   light

one eye on   apiece
of tasty

           trash
being the crux

        waiting on the light
like a crow might   know

in the ruined rhyme   of us

is the crux is

                    '

if a crow—

then an ice cube con-
            structed
of black ice

Then the mild   or immense
accomplishments

            of the radish bone de-
pending on weather
            you look—

The black ice   is growing
like tubers under-
                        ground

     sneaking up   to the
surface   every morning

to eat   the sunlight

(to irridesce)

‘

And if out— one luxated

      window, one then looks—

to see   at the side of the road:
a crow tangling
      with   the text—

So as to true
      the obligation—

You must
fallow thru
     with what

         you've begun—

Acknowledgements

Some of these poems first appeared in *Posit, Denver Quarterly, Poet Lore, Bennington Review, VOLT, Columba, Sixth Finch*, and *Sprung Formal*— endless thanks to the editors of those journals for their support, especially: Alicia Wright, Susan Lewis, Austin Rodenbiker, Benjamin Garcia, Gillian Conoley.

My love and gratitude—to fahima ife, Brian Teare, and especially Ruth Ellen Kocher for selecting this manuscript—to Alana, who is the beginning of this book—to Laura Mullen, Olivia Muenz, Sam Bickford, Elizabeth Kolenda, Katherine Hur, Ava Hofmann, Chris Barrett, Lara Glenum—to Rusty Morrison and Laura Joakimson, and all at Omnidawn—and to Clara...

Ian U Lockaby is a poet, translator, and editor of the journal *mercury firs*. His work has been published in journals such as *Kenyon Review*, *Denver Quarterly*, *Ecotone*, and *Poetry Northwest*. For many years he lived in and around Olympia, WA, where he worked on vegetable farms. He now lives in New Orleans.

Defensible Space / if a crow—
by Ian U Lockaby
Cover art: "Linnae Slash Pile" by Clara DeWeese
Cover design by Ian U Lockaby
Cover typeface: copperplate gothic and didot
Interior design by Sophia Carr and Laura Joakimson
Interior typeface: garamond premier pro

Printed in the United States
by Books International,
Dulles, Virginia on Acid Free Archival Quality Recycled Paper

Publication of this book was made possible in part by gifts from Katherine &
John Gravendyk in honor of Hillary Gravendyk,
Francesca Bell, Mary Mackey, and The New Place Fund

Omnidawn Publishing Oakland, California
Staff and Volunteers, Fall 2024
Rusty Morrison & Laura Joakimson, co-publishers
Rob Hendricks, poetry & fiction editor,
& post-pub marketing
Jeffrey Kingman, copy editor
Sharon Zetter, poetry editor & book designer
Anthony Cody, poetry editor
Liza Flum, poetry editor
Kimberly Reyes, poetry editor
Elizabeth Aeschliman, fiction & poetry editor
Jennifer Metsker, marketing assistant
Katie Tomzynski, marketing assistant
Kailey Garcia, marketing assistant
Sophia Carr, production editor